TROMBONE

MOVIE FAVORITES

Solos and Band Arrangements
Correlated with Essential Elements Band Method

Arranged by
MICHAEL SWEENEY

Welcome to Essential Elements Movie Favorites! There are two versions of each selection in this versatile book. The SOLO version appears on the left-hand page of your book. The FULL BAND arrangement appears on the right-hand page. Optional accompaniment recordings are available separately in CD or cassette format. Use these recordings when playing solos for friends and family.

ISBN 978-0-7935-5955-8

HAL•LEONARD®
CORPORATION

7777 W. BLUEMOUND RD. P.O. BOX 13819 MILWAUKEE, WI 53213

00860011

From The Universal Motion Picture JURASSIC PARK

Theme From "JURASSIC PARK"

TROMBONE
Solo

Composed by JOHN WILLIAMS
Arranged by MICHAEL SWEENEY

00860011

MCA music publishing

From The Universal Motion Picture JURASSIC PARK

Theme From "JURASSIC PARK"

Composed by JOHN WILLIAMS
Arranged by MICHAEL SWEENEY

TROMBONE
Band Arrangement

MCA music publishing

00860011

From CHARIOTS OF FIRE

CHARIOTS OF FIRE

Music by VANGELIS
Arranged by MICHAEL SWEENEY

TROMBONE
Solo

00860011

CHARIOTS OF FIRE

Music by VANGELIS
Arranged by MICHAEL SWEENEY

TROMBONE
Band Arrangement

00860011

From **THE MAN FROM SNOWY RIVER**

THE MAN FROM SNOWY RIVER

(Main Title Theme)

By BRUCE ROWLAND

Arranged by MICHAEL SWEENEY

TROMBONE
Solo

From THE MAN FROM SNOWY RIVER

THE MAN FROM SNOWY RIVER

(Main Title Theme)

By BRUCE ROWLAND
Arranged by MICHAEL SWEENEY

TROMBONE
Band Arrangement

00860011

From The Paramount Motion Picture FORREST GUMP

FORREST GUMP - MAIN TITLE

(Feather Theme)

Music by ALAN SILVESTRI
Arranged by MICHAEL SWEENEY

TROMBONE
Solo

00860011

FORREST GUMP - MAIN TITLE

From The Paramount Motion Picture FORREST GUMP

(Feather Theme)

Music by ALAN SILVESTRI
Arranged by MICHAEL SWEENEY

TROMBONE
Band Arrangement

00860011

From AN AMERICAN TAIL
SOMEWHERE OUT THERE

Words and Music by JAMES HORNER,
BARRY MANN and CYNTHIA WEIL
Arranged by MICHAEL SWEENEY

TROMBONE
Solo

MCA music publishing

SOMEWHERE OUT THERE

Words and Music by JAMES HORNER,
BARRY MANN and CYNTHIA WEIL
Arranged by MICHAEL SWEENEY

TROMBONE
Band Arrangement

Moderately Slow

MCA music publishing

From **DANCES WITH WOLVES**
THE JOHN DUNBAR THEME

By JOHN BARRY
Arranged by MICHAEL SWEENEY

TROMBONE
Solo

From **DANCES WITH WOLVES**
THE JOHN DUNBAR THEME

TROMBONE
Band Arrangement

By JOHN BARRY
Arranged by MICHAEL SWEENEY

00860011

From The Paramount Motion Picture RAIDERS OF THE LOST ARK

RAIDERS MARCH

By JOHN WILLIAMS
Arranged by MICHAEL SWEENEY

TROMBONE
Solo

From The Paramount Motion Picture RAIDERS OF THE LOST ARK
RAIDERS MARCH

TROMBONE
Band Arrangement

By JOHN WILLIAMS
Arranged by MICHAEL SWEENEY

00860011

From APOLLO 13
APOLLO 13
(End Credits)

By JAMES HORNER
Arranged by MICHAEL SWEENEY

TROMBONE
Solo

00860011

MCA music publishing

APOLLO 13
(End Credits)

By JAMES HORNER
Arranged by MICHAEL SWEENEY

TROMBONE
Band Arrangement

MCA music publishing

00860011

From The Universal Picture E.T. (THE EXTRA-TERRESTRIAL)

THEME FROM E.T. (THE EXTRA-TERRESTRIAL)

TROMBONE
Solo

Music by JOHN WILLIAMS
Arranged by MICHAEL SWEENEY

MCA music publishing

THEME FROM E.T. (THE EXTRA-TERRESTRIAL)

TROMBONE
Band Arrangement

Music by JOHN WILLIAMS
Arranged by MICHAEL SWEENEY

MCA music publishing

Theme From The Paramount Picture STAR TREK

STAR TREK®-THE MOTION PICTURE

Music by JERRY GOLDSMITH
Arranged by MICHAEL SWEENEY

TROMBONE
Solo

Theme From The Paramount Picture STAR TREK

STAR TREK®-THE MOTION PICTURE

TROMBONE
Band Arrangement

Music by JERRY GOLDSMITH
Arranged by MICHAEL SWEENEY

00860011

From The Universal Motion Picture BACK TO THE FUTURE

BACK TO THE FUTURE

TROMBONE
Solo

By ALAN SILVESTRI
Arranged by MICHAEL SWEENEY

MCA music publishing

BACK TO THE FUTURE

By ALAN SILVESTRI
Arranged by MICHAEL SWEENEY

TROMBONE
Band Arrangement

MCA music publishing